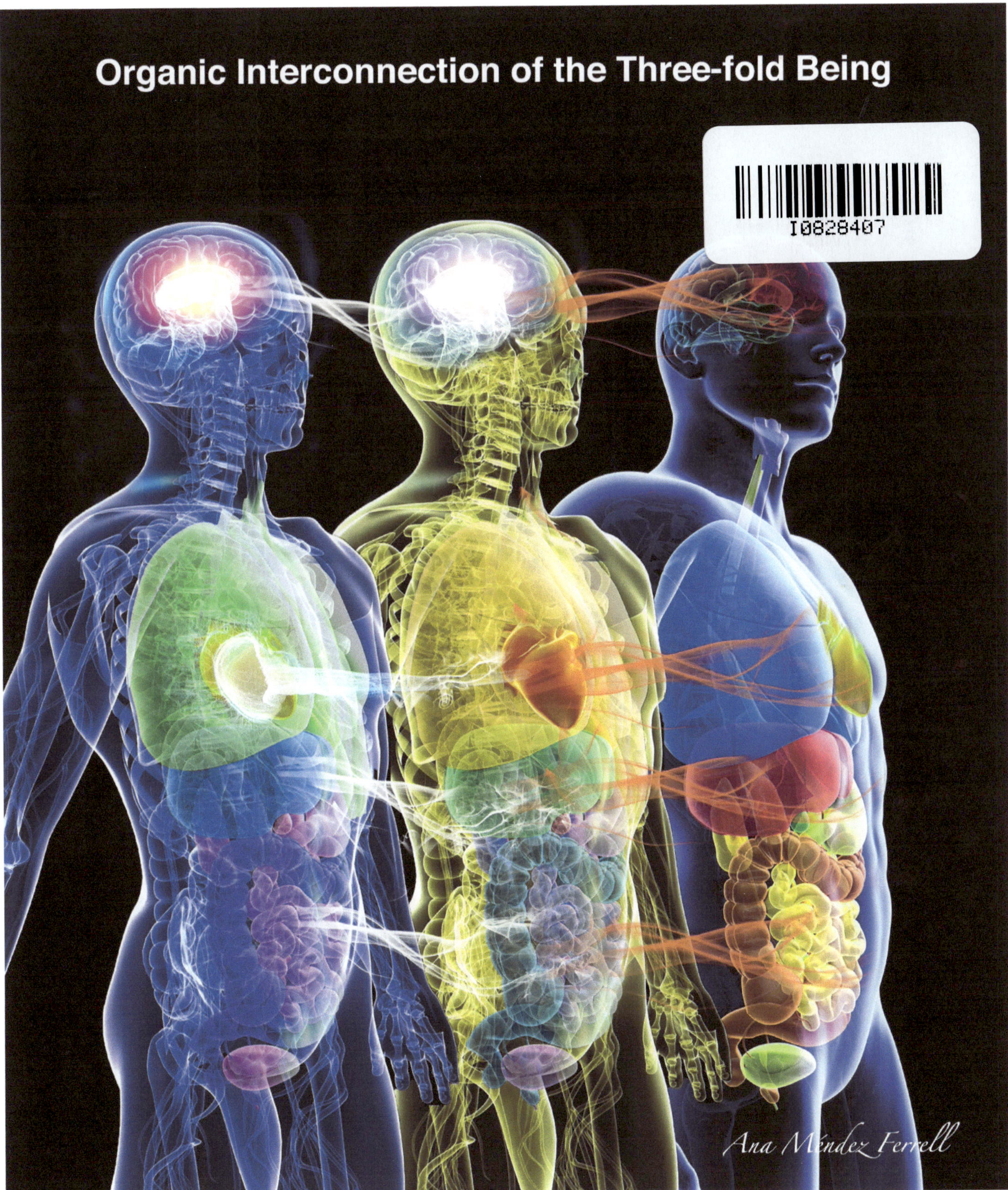

Organic Interconnection of the Three Fold Being

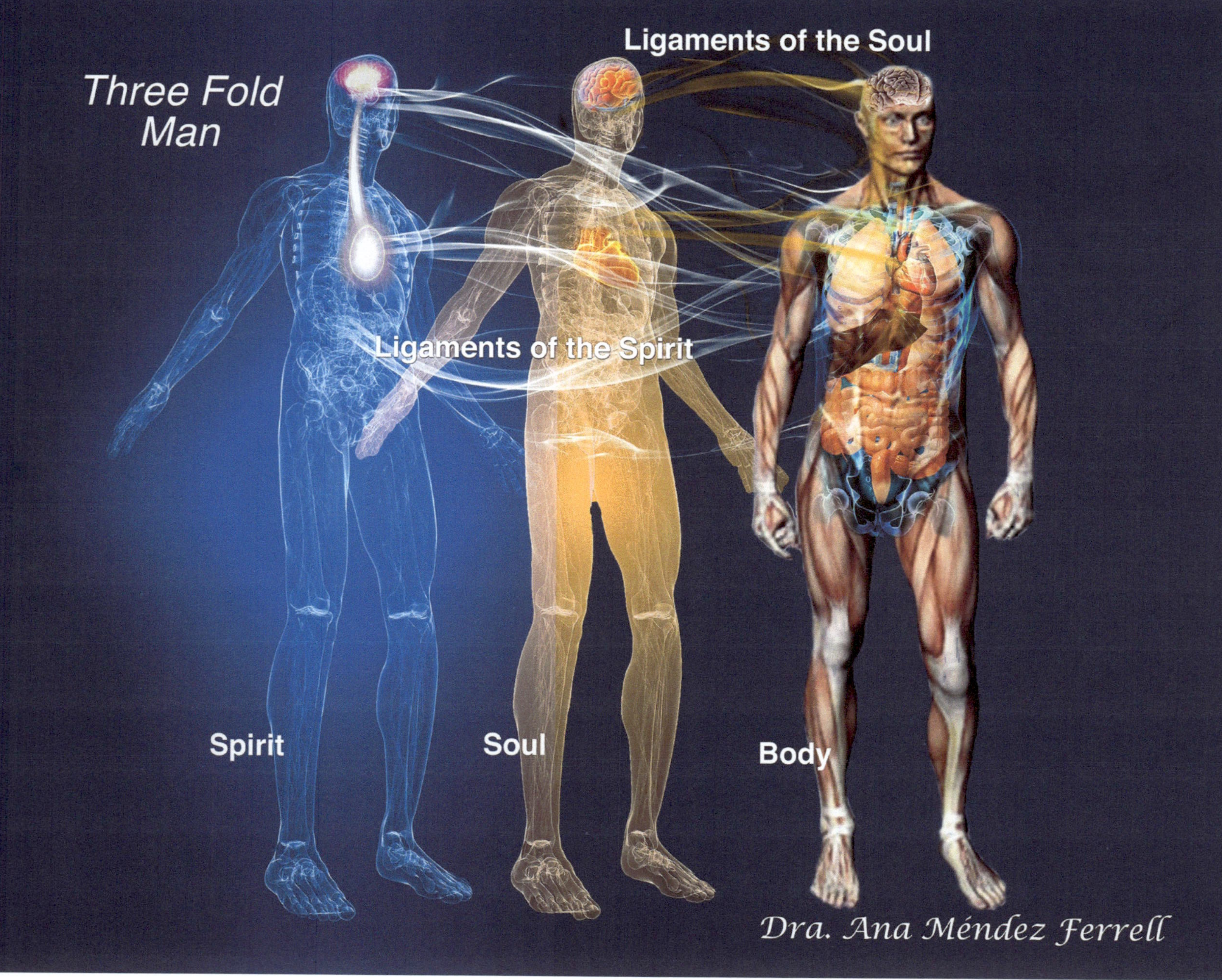
Three Fold
Man
Ligaments of the Soul
Ligaments of the Spirit
Spirit
Soul
Body
Dra. Ana Méndez Ferrell

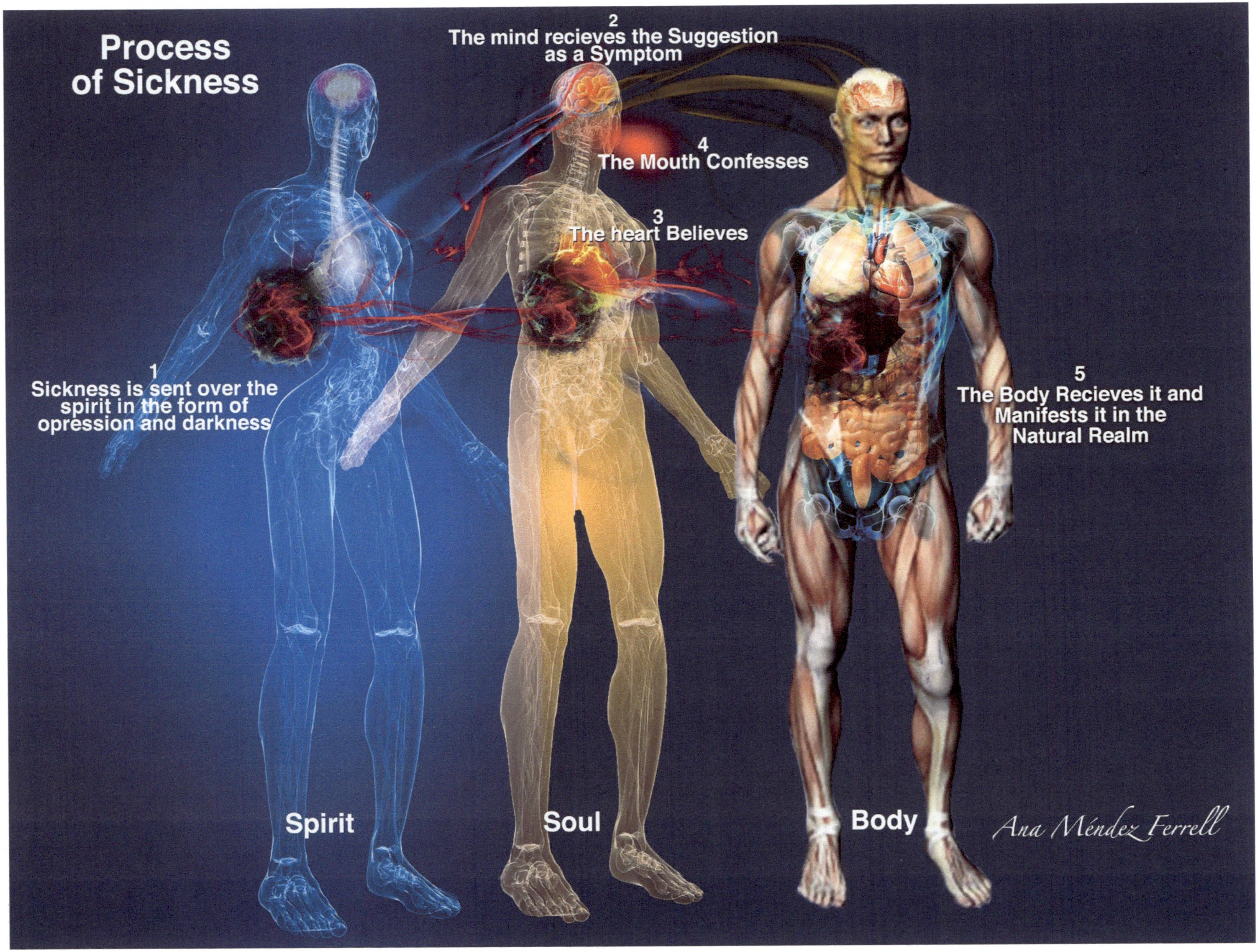

Process of Sickness

1
Sickness is sent over the spirit in the form of opression and darkness

2
The mind recieves the Suggestion as a Symptom

3
The heart Believes

4
The Mouth Confesses

5
The Body Recieves it and Manifests it in the Natural Realm

Spirit

Soul

Body

Ana Méndez Ferrell

Process of Sickness

The Living Creature in the Vision of Ezekiel

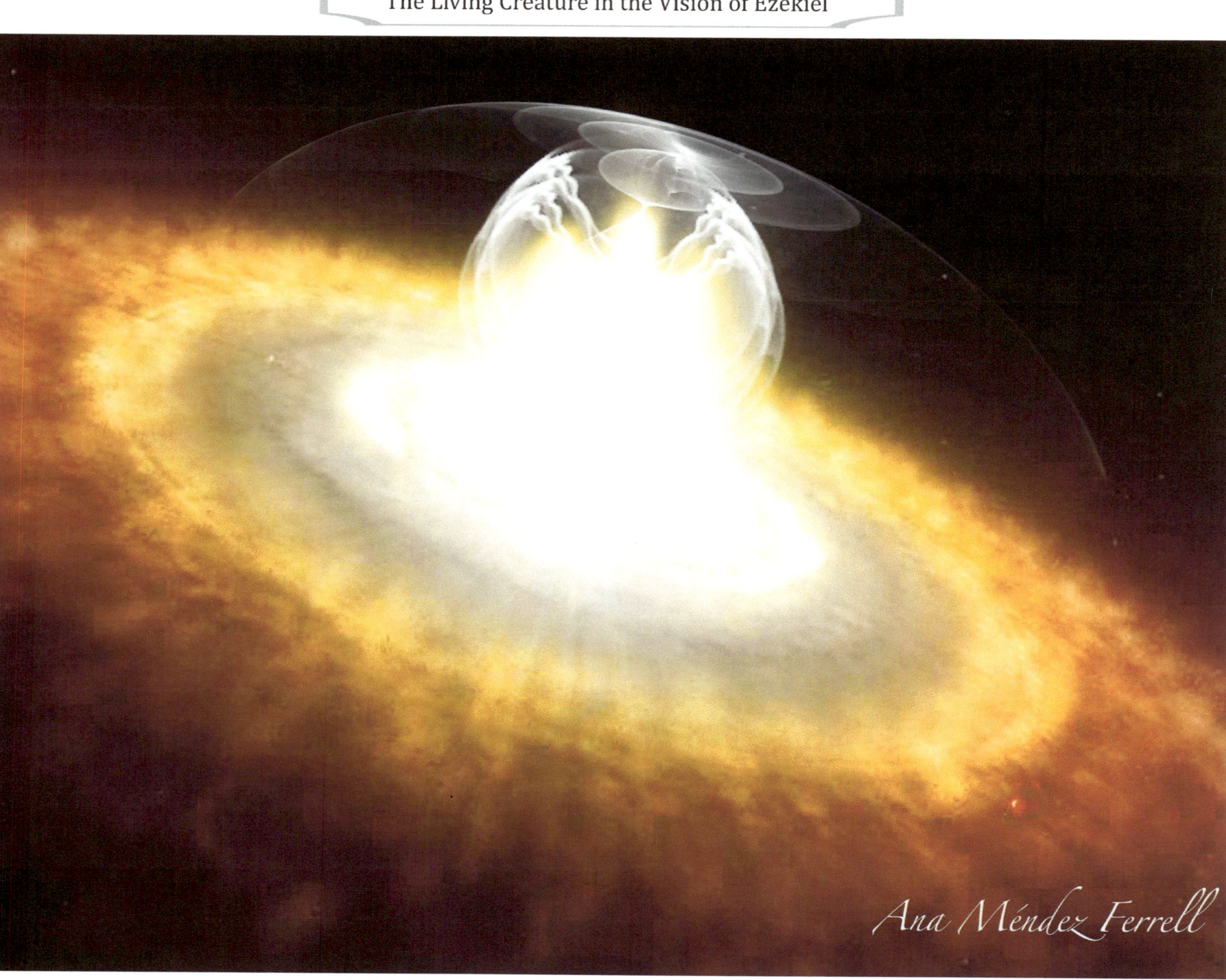

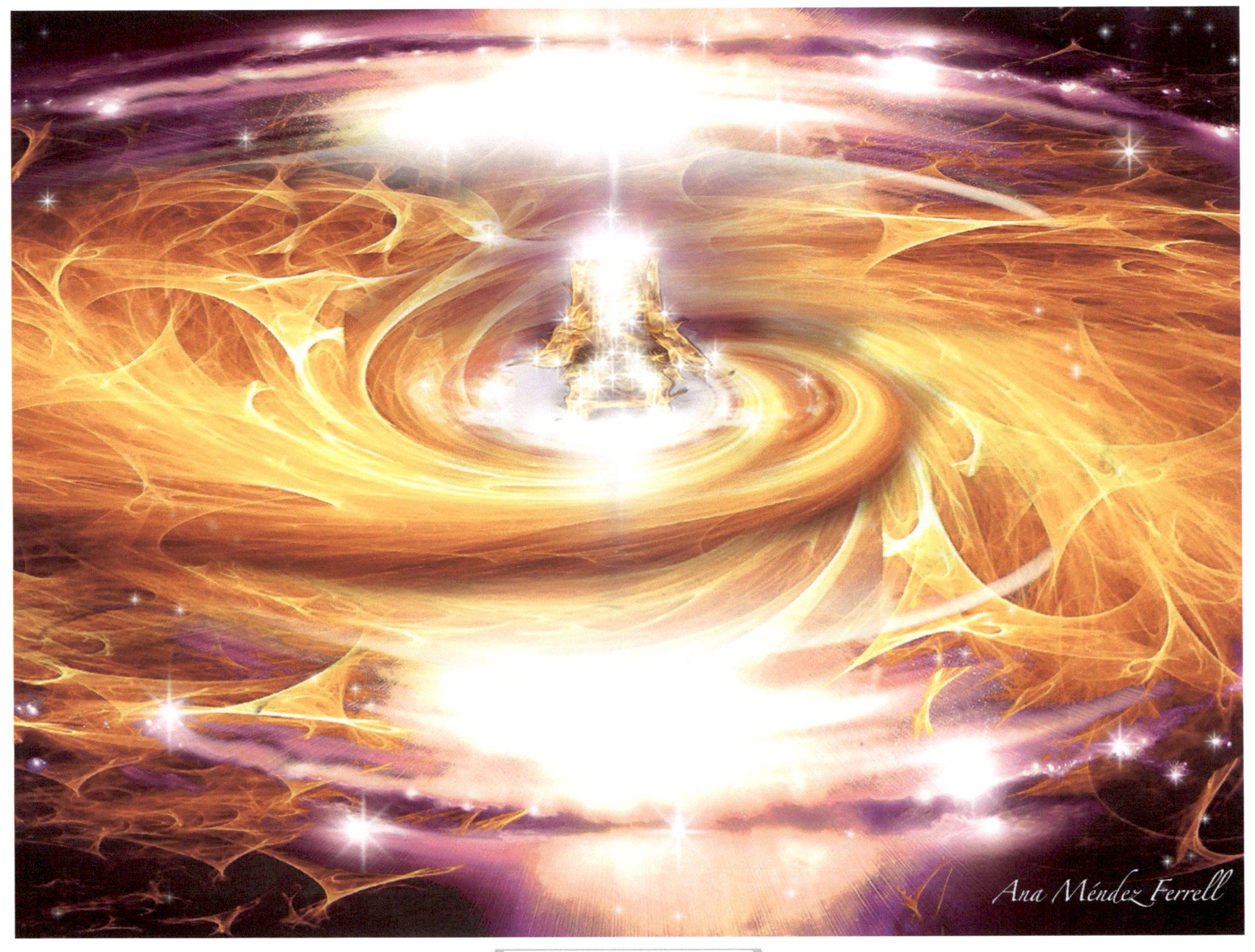

The Throne of God

Central View of the Seven Spirits

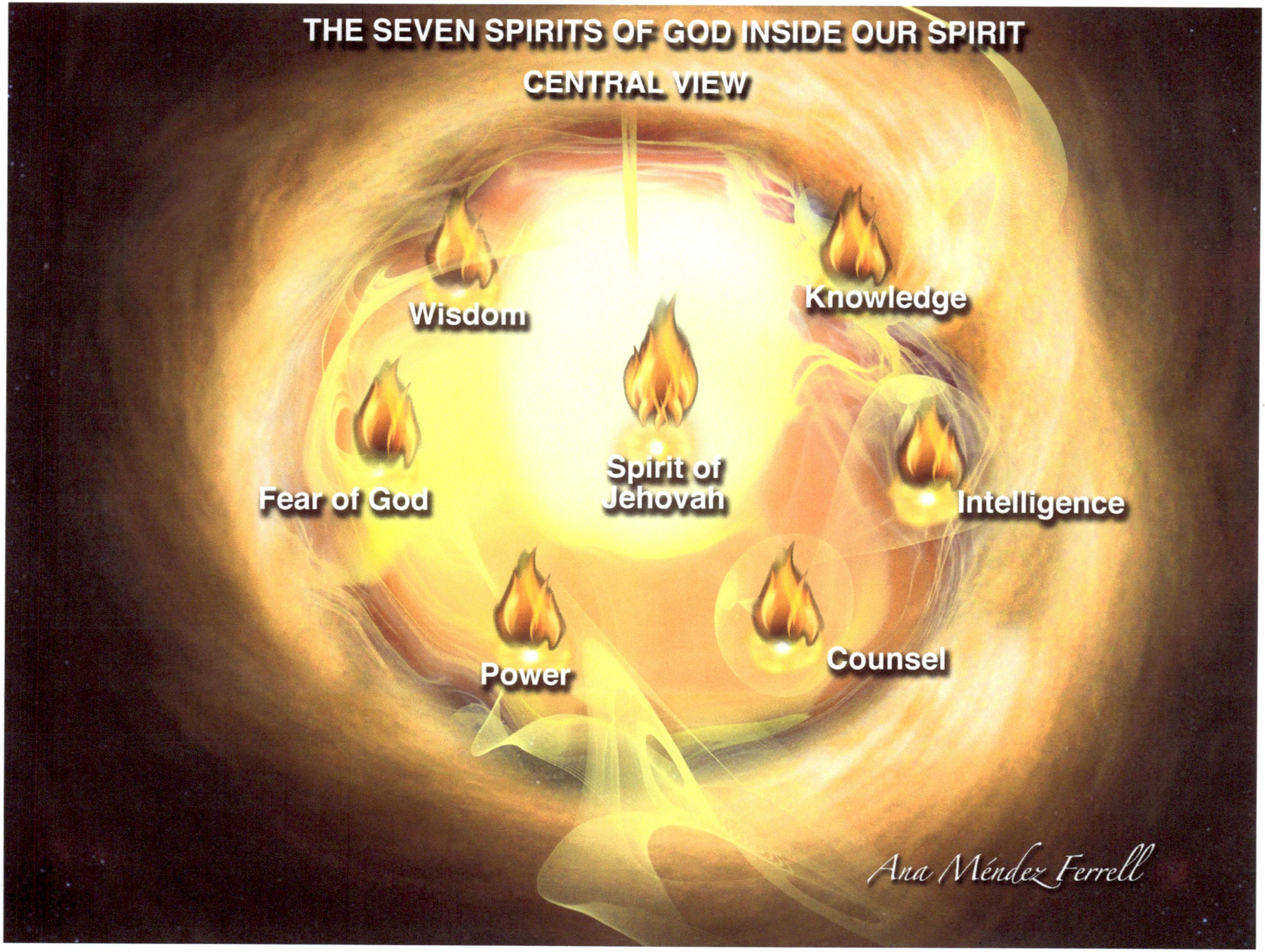

THE SEVEN SPIRITS OF GOD INSIDE OUR SPIRIT

CENTRAL VIEW

Wisdom

Knowledge

Spirit of Jehovah

Fear of God

Intelligence

Power

Counsel

Ana Méndez Ferrell

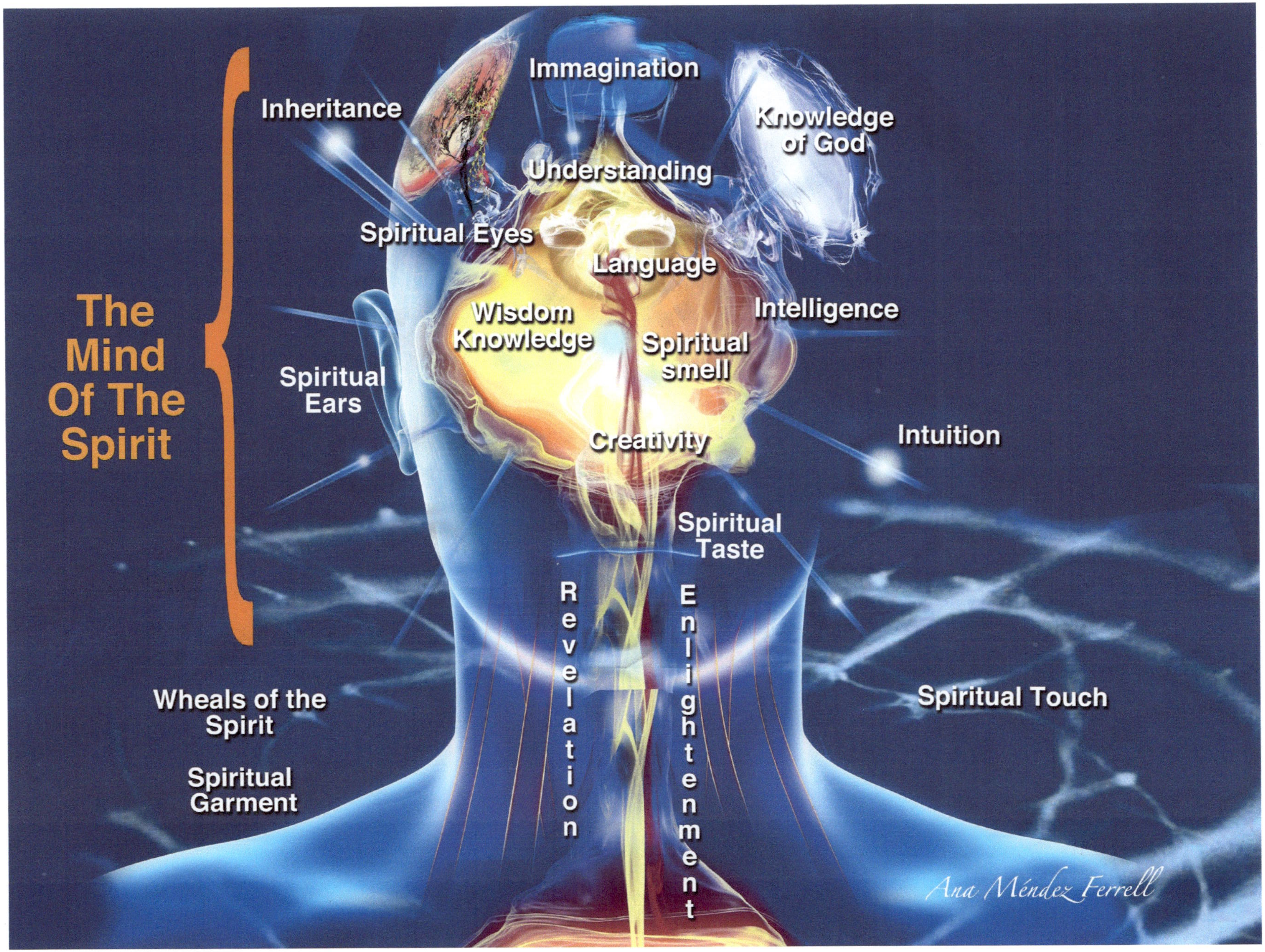

Mind of the Spirit

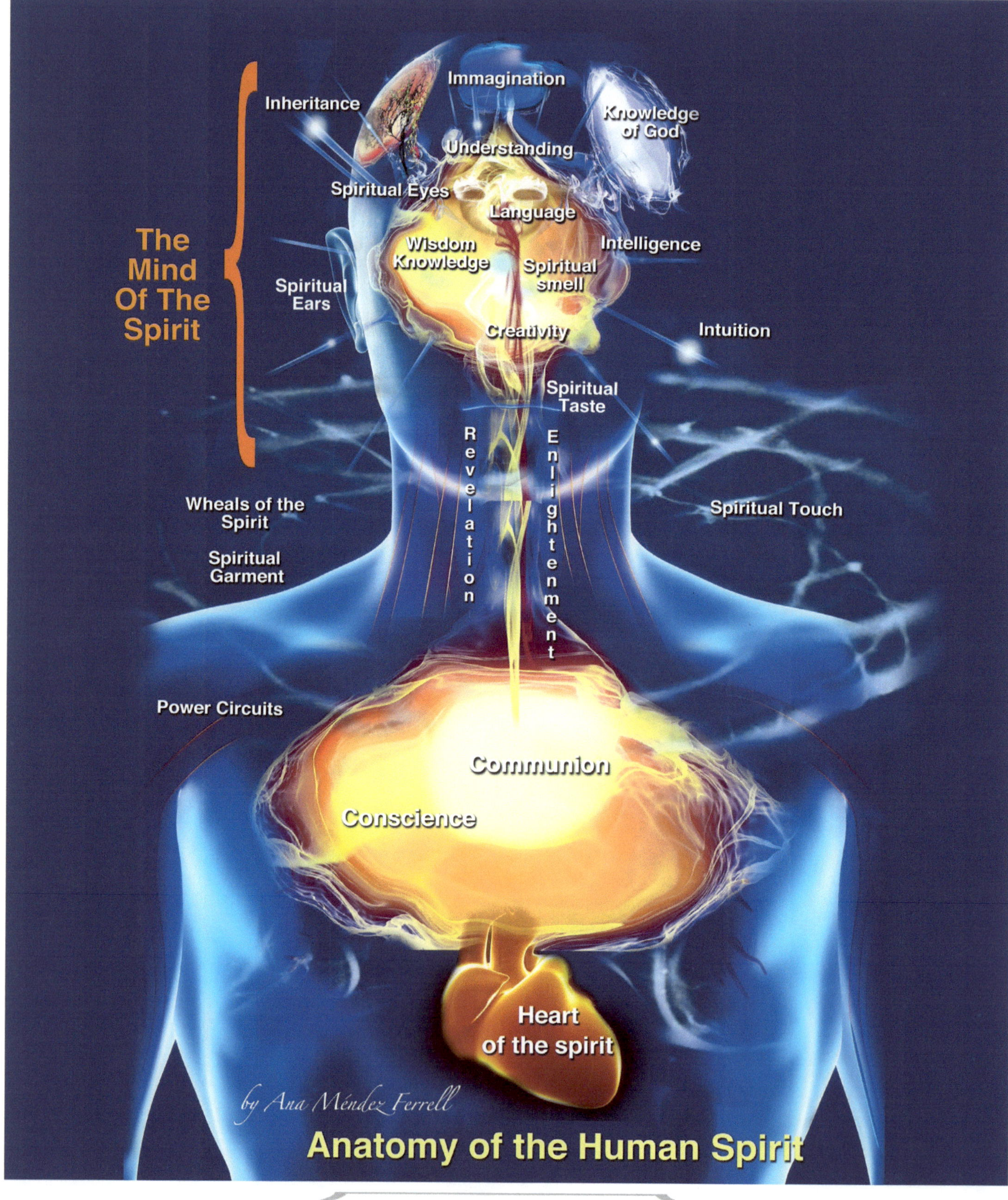

Anatomy of the Human Spirit

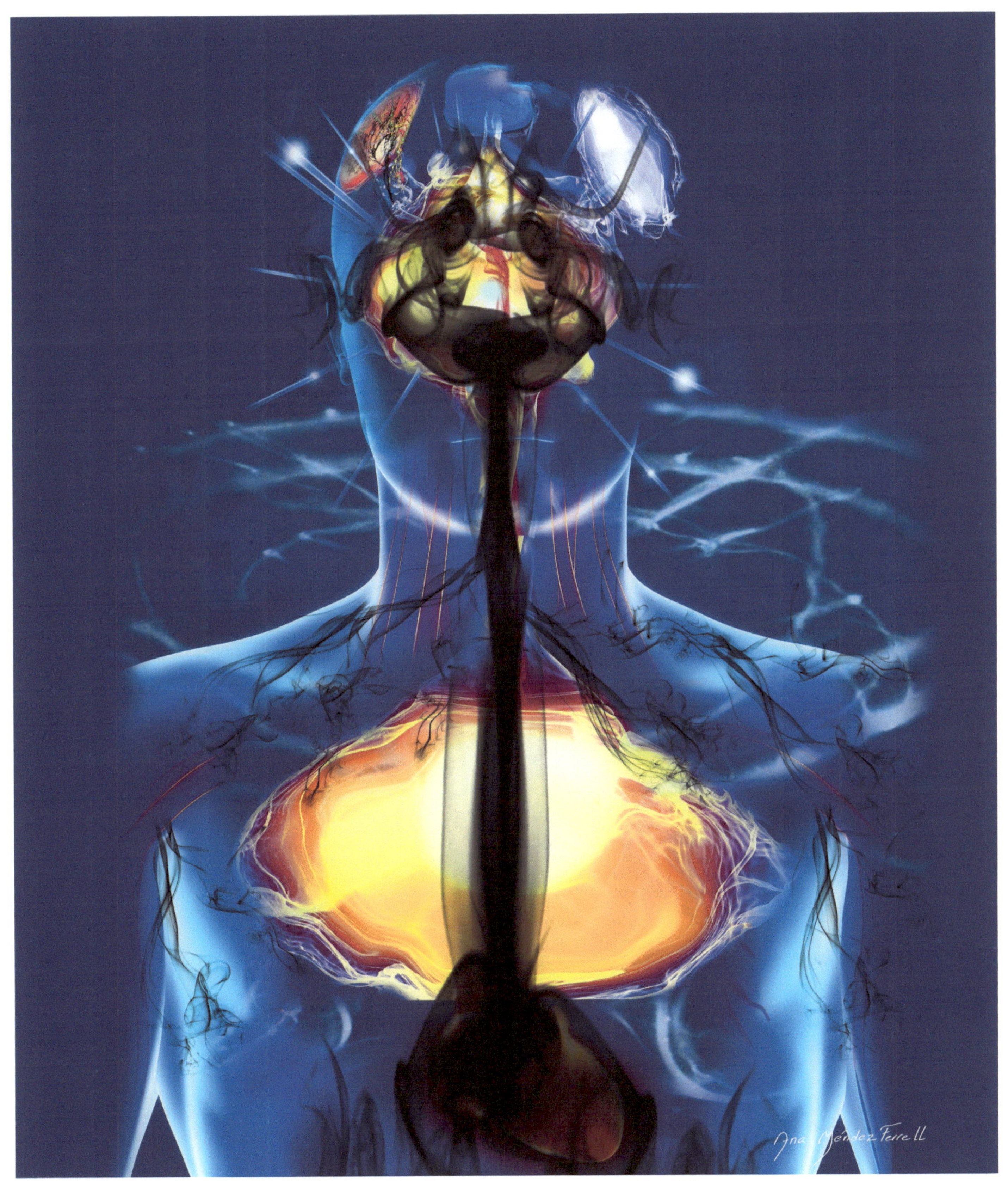

The Spirit Contaminated by Iniquity

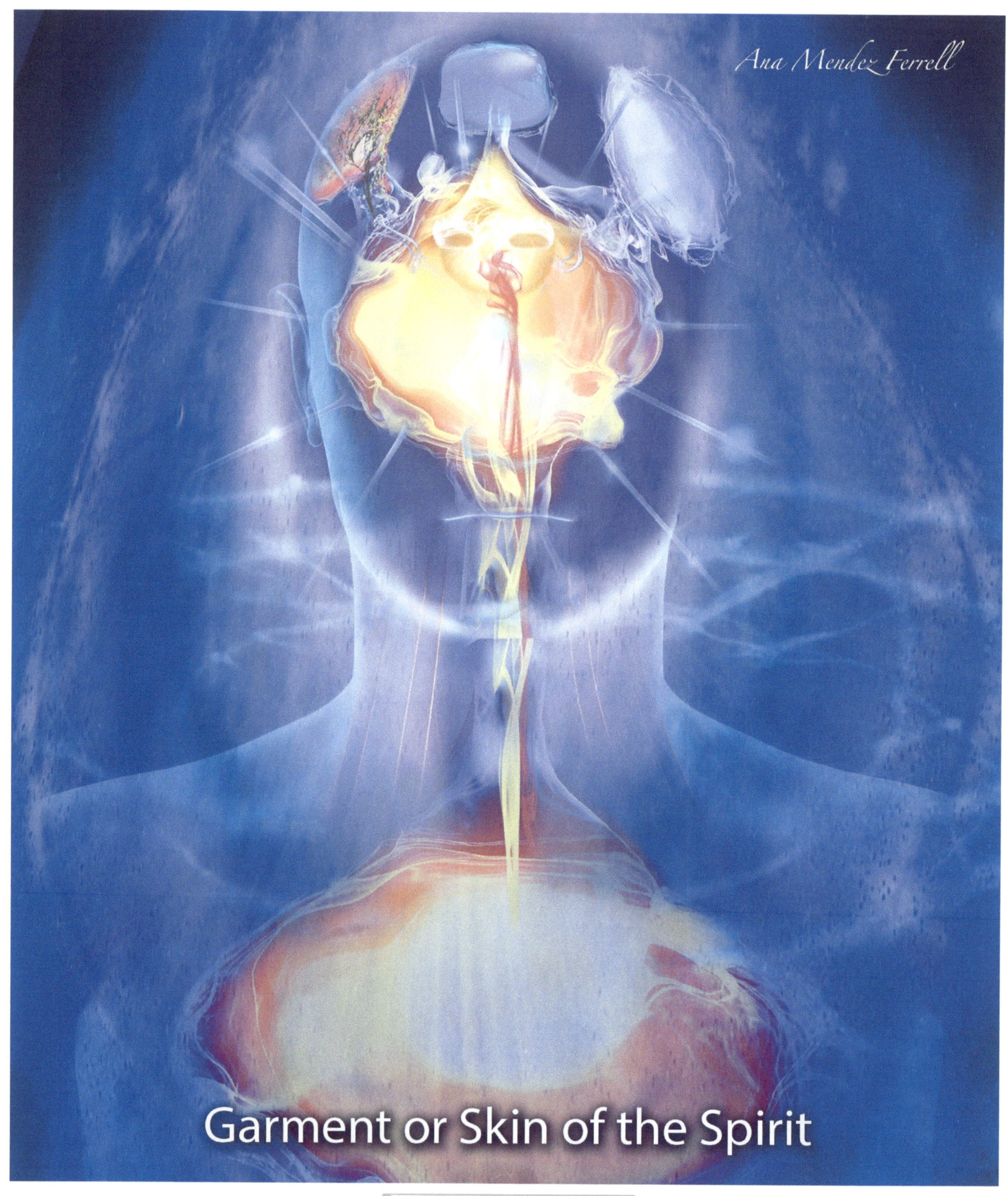
Ana Mendez Ferrell
Garment or Skin of the Spirit

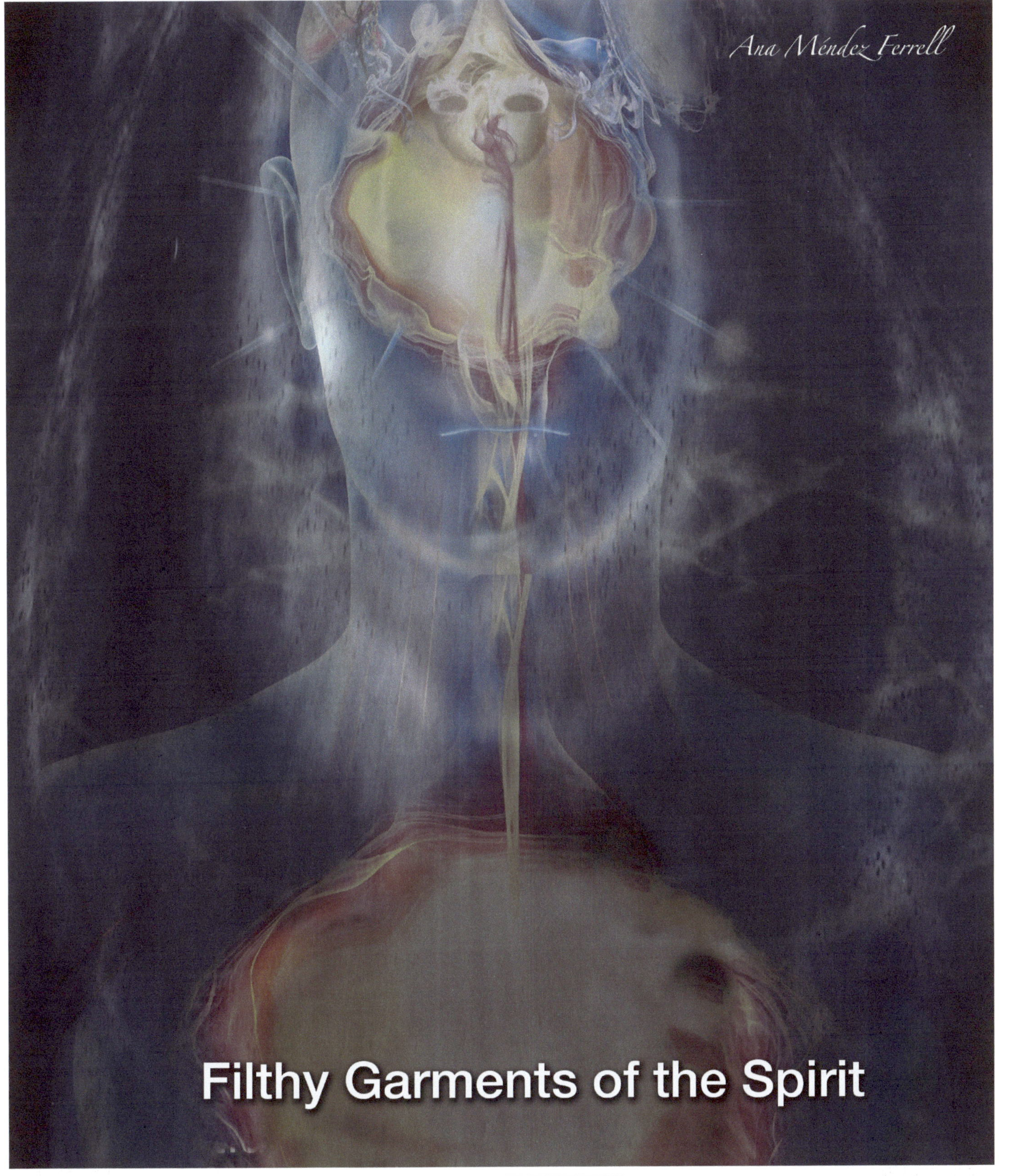
Ana Méndez Ferrell
Filthy Garments of the Spirit

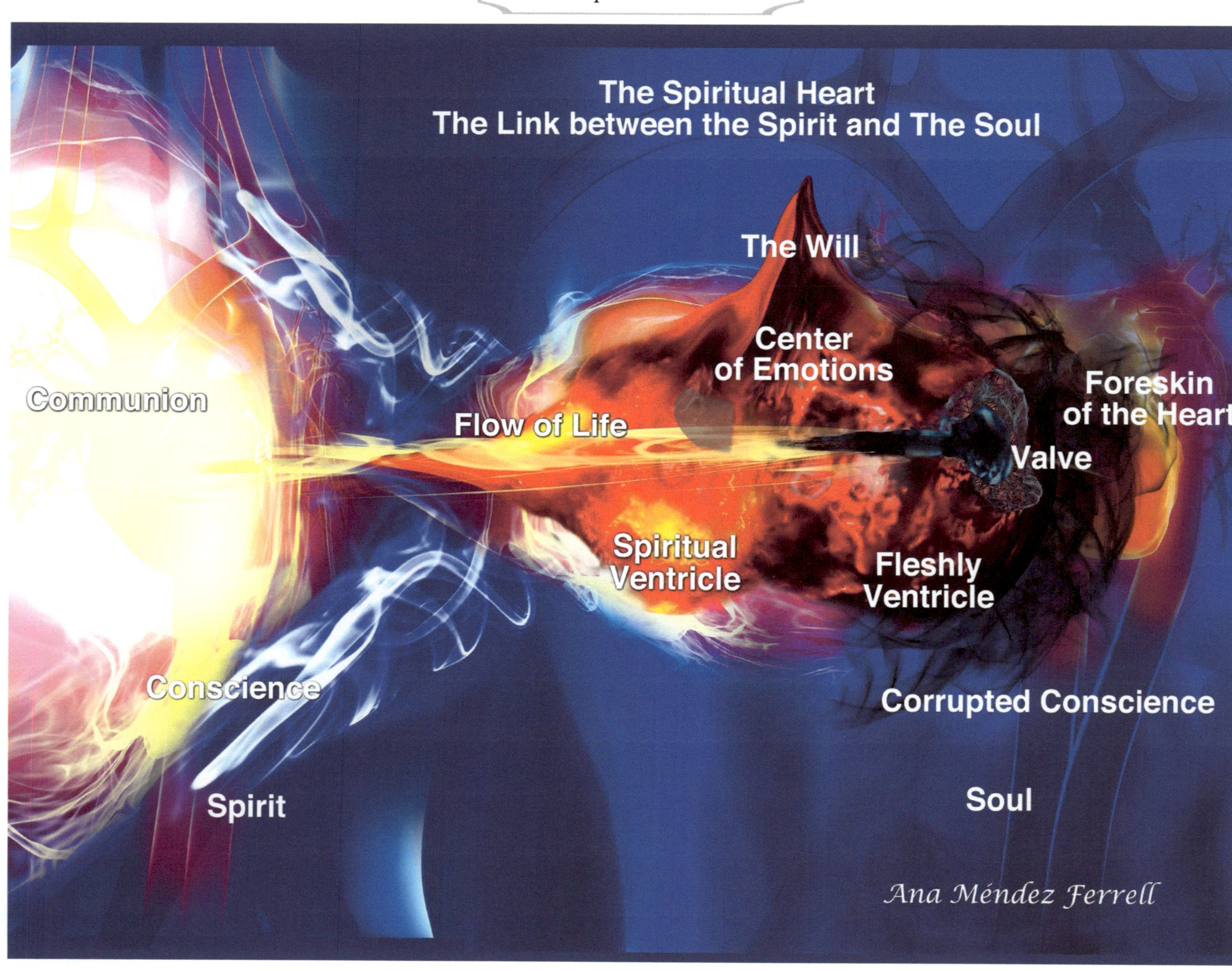
The Spiritual Heart
The Link between the Spirit and The Soul
The Will
Center of Emotions
Communion
Flow of Life
Foreskin of the Heart
Valve
Spiritual Ventricle
Fleshly Ventricle
Conscience
Corrupted Conscience
Spirit
Soul
Ana Méndez Ferrell

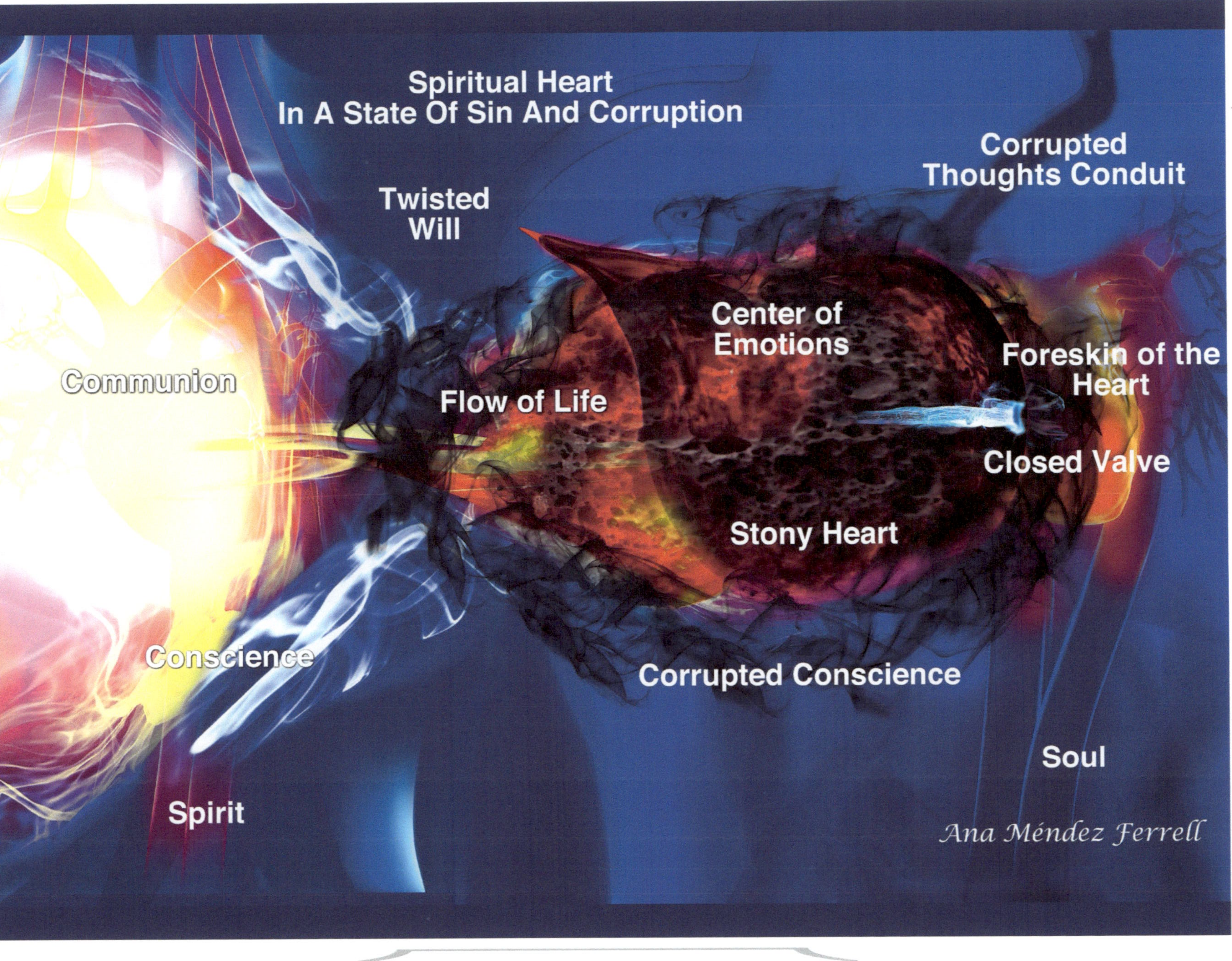

The Spiritual Heart Corrupted by Sin

Spiritual Heart According to God

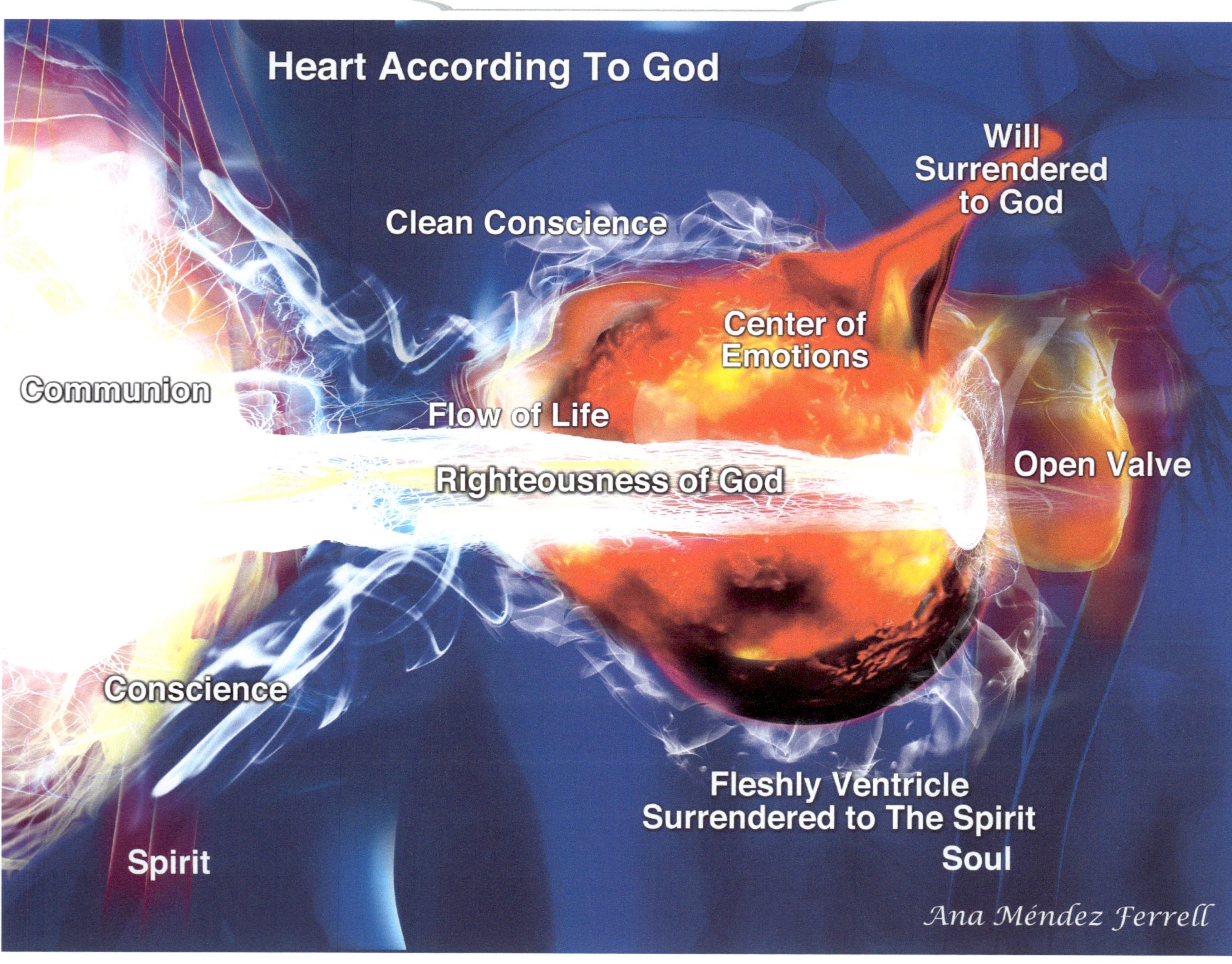

Sectional view
of the Open
Valve

With its ability to see
into the Kingdom of
God and to transmit
eternal life from the
Communion center

Ana Méndez Ferrell

Government Of The Soul

Ana Méndez Ferrell

Non Regenerated Soul

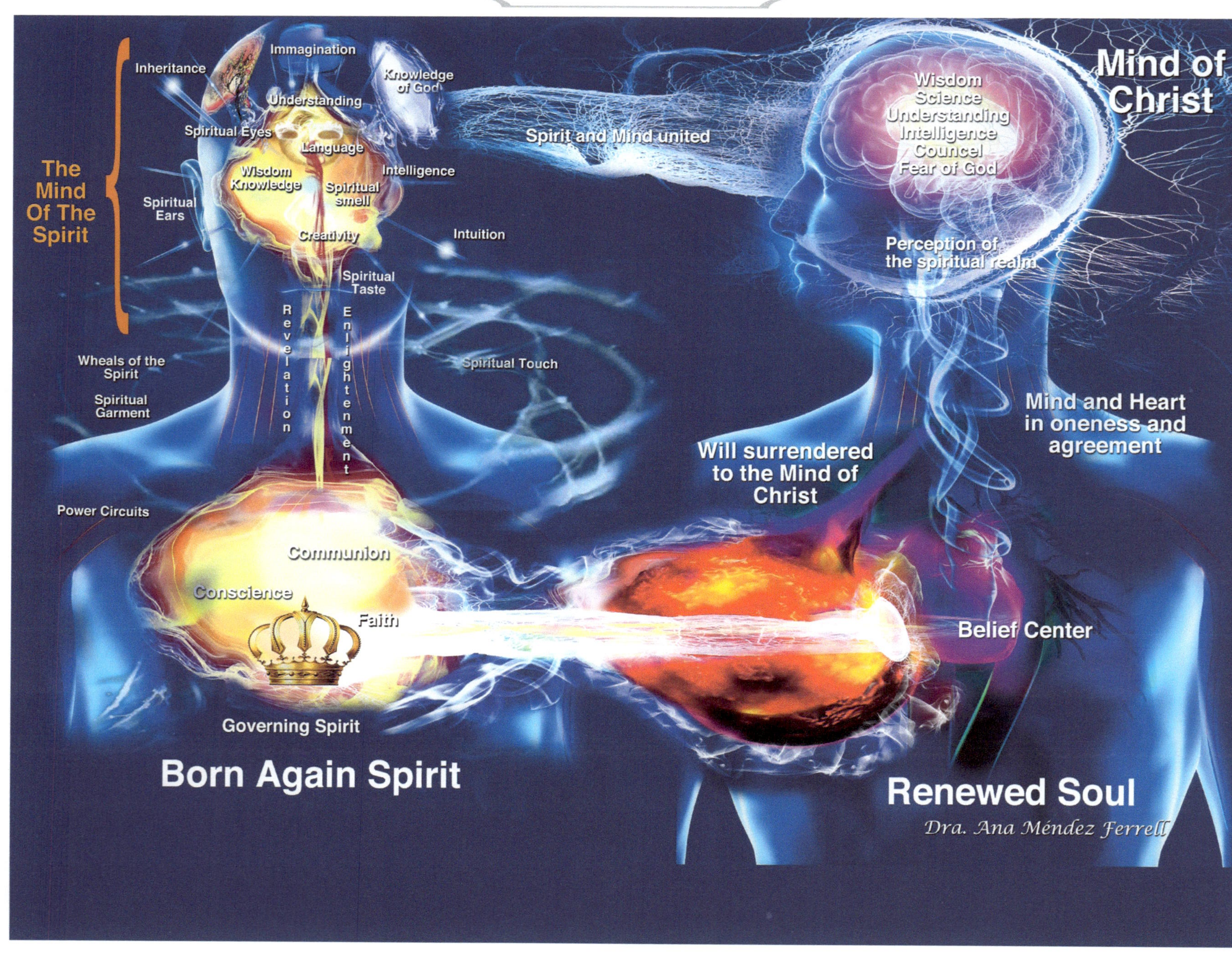
The Mind Of The Spirit
Inheritance
Immagination
Knowledge of God
Understanding
Spiritual Eyes
Language
Wisdom Knowledge
Spiritual smell
Intelligence
Spiritual Ears
Creativity
Intuition
Spiritual Taste
Revelation
Enlightenment
Spiritual Touch
Wheals of the Spirit
Spiritual Garment
Power Circuits
Communion
Conscience
Faith
Governing Spirit
Born Again Spirit
Spirit and Mind united
Mind of Christ
Wisdom
Science
Understanding
Intelligence
Councel
Fear of God
Perception of the spiritual realm
Mind and Heart in oneness and agreement
Will surrendered to the Mind of Christ
Belief Center
Renewed Soul
Dra. Ana Méndez Ferrell

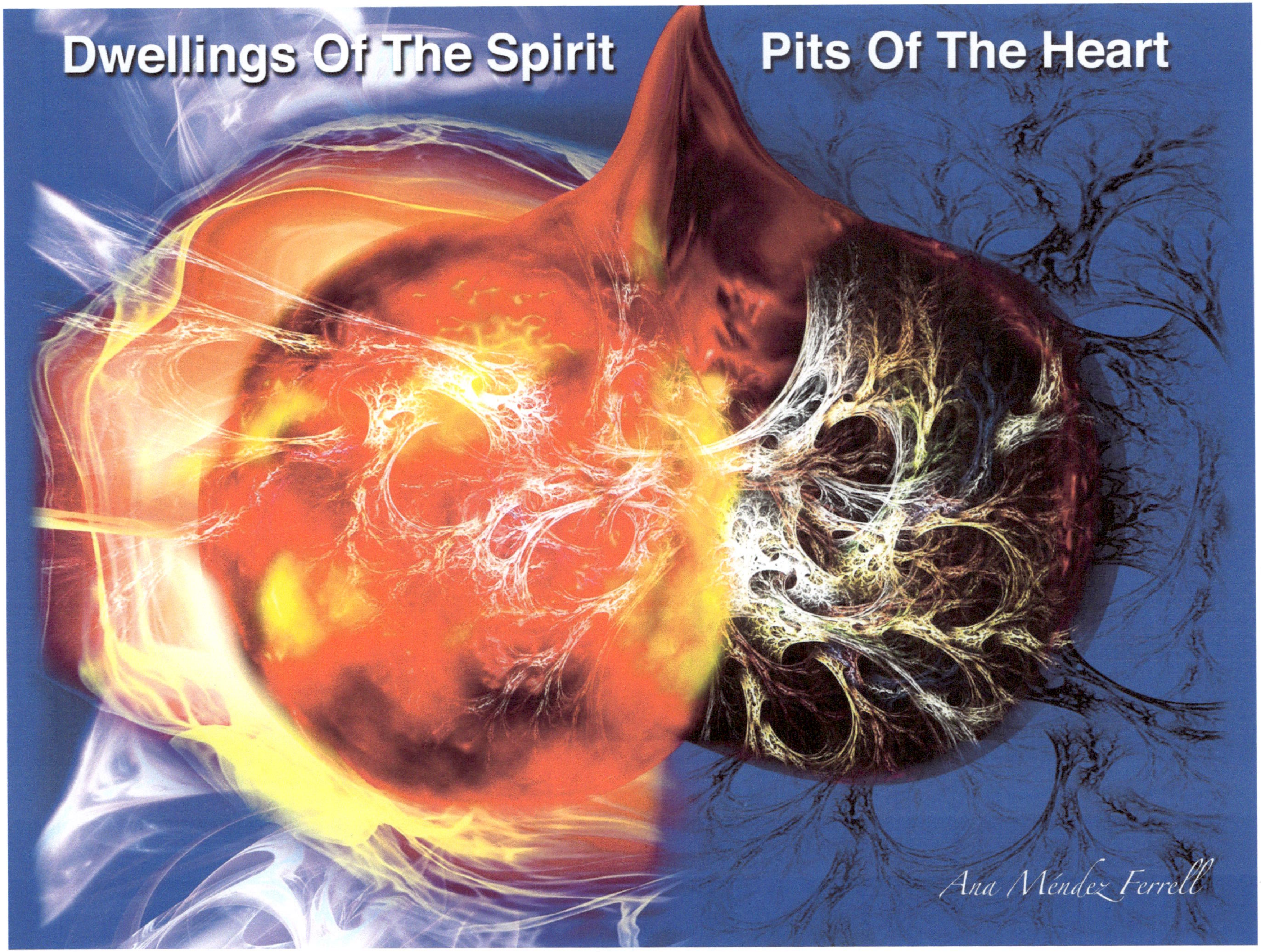

Dwellings Of The Spirit

Pits Of The Heart

Ana Méndez Ferrell

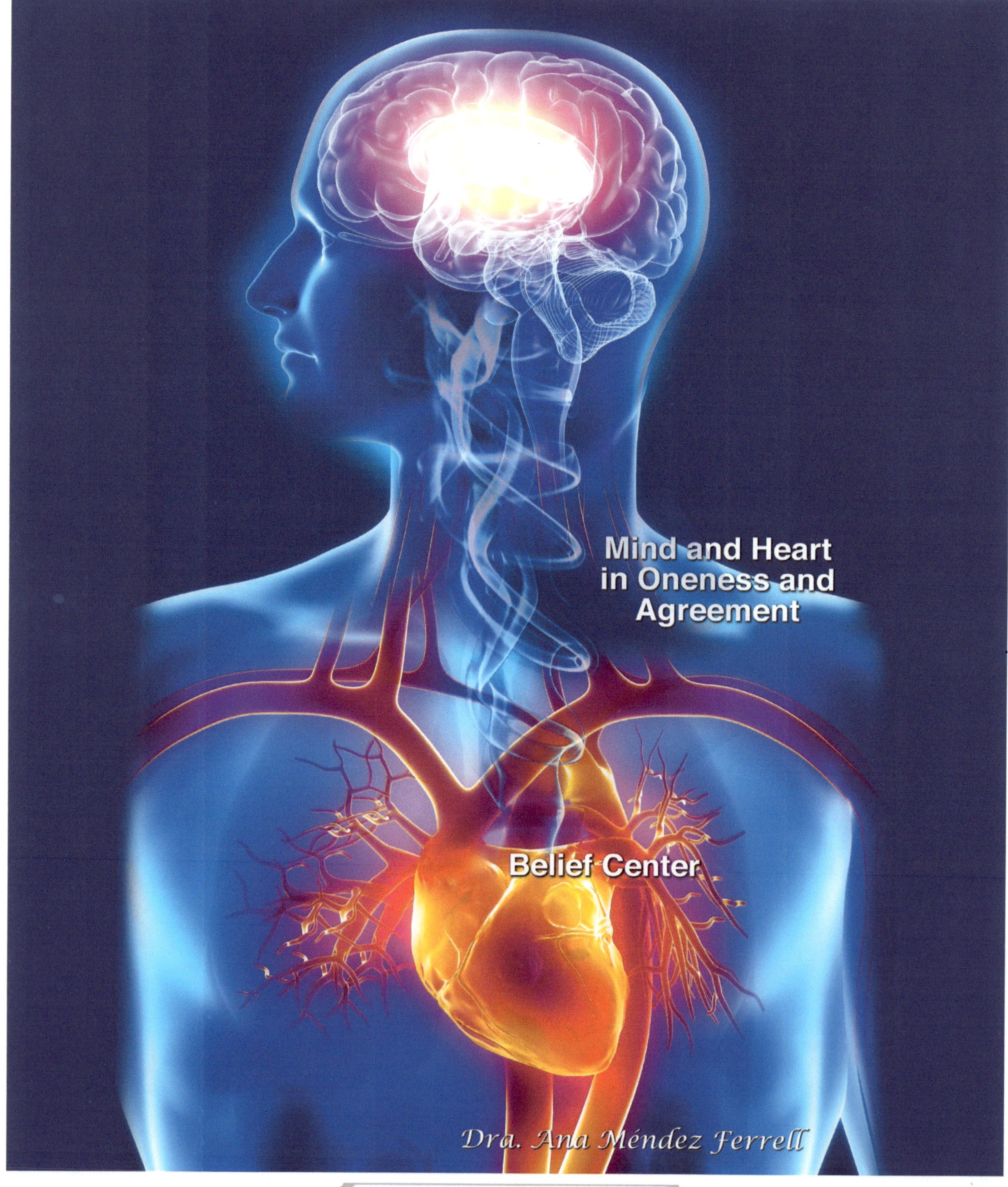

Mind and Heart in Agreement

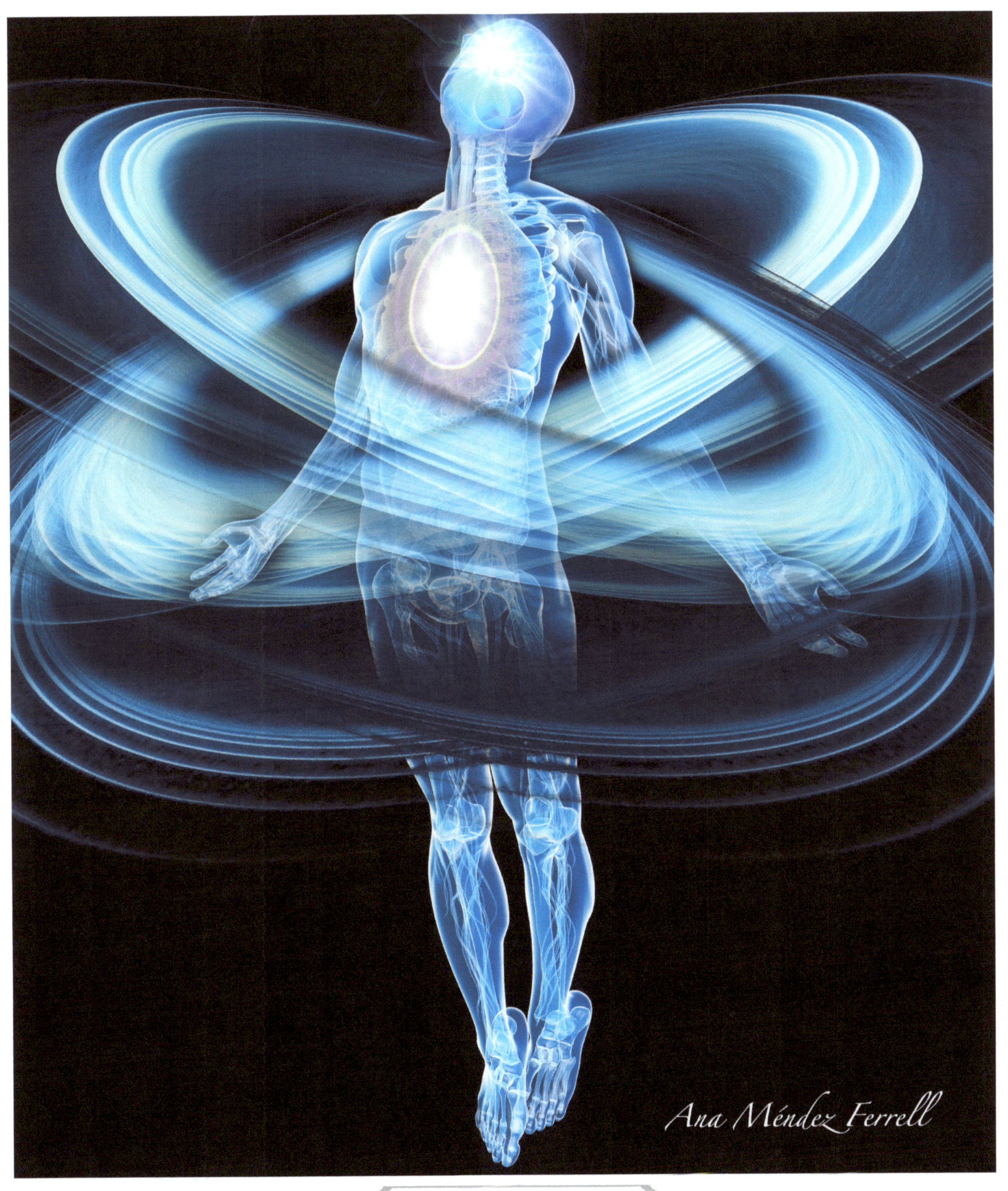

The Wheels of the Spirit

Dra.Ana Méndez Ferrell

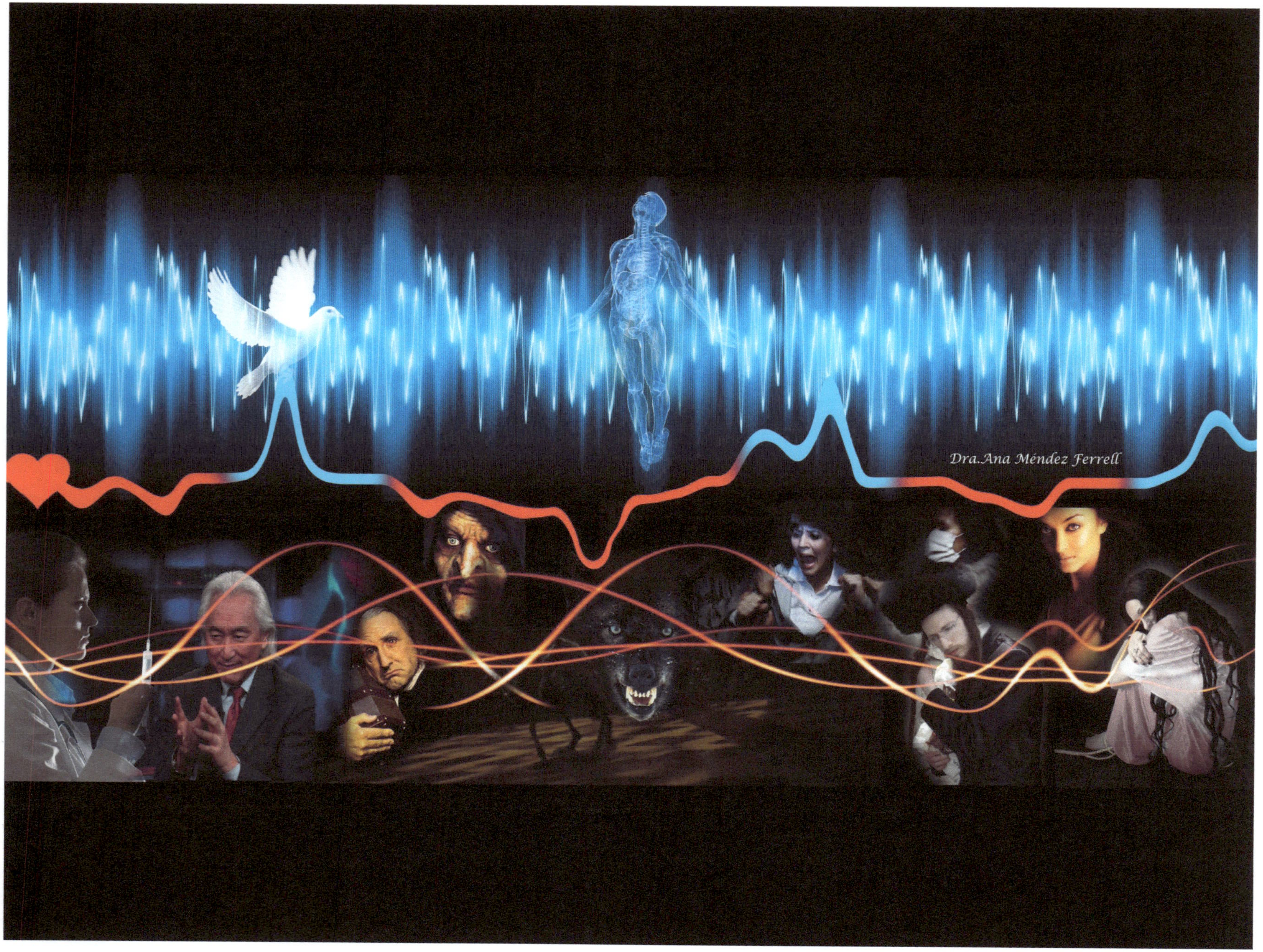

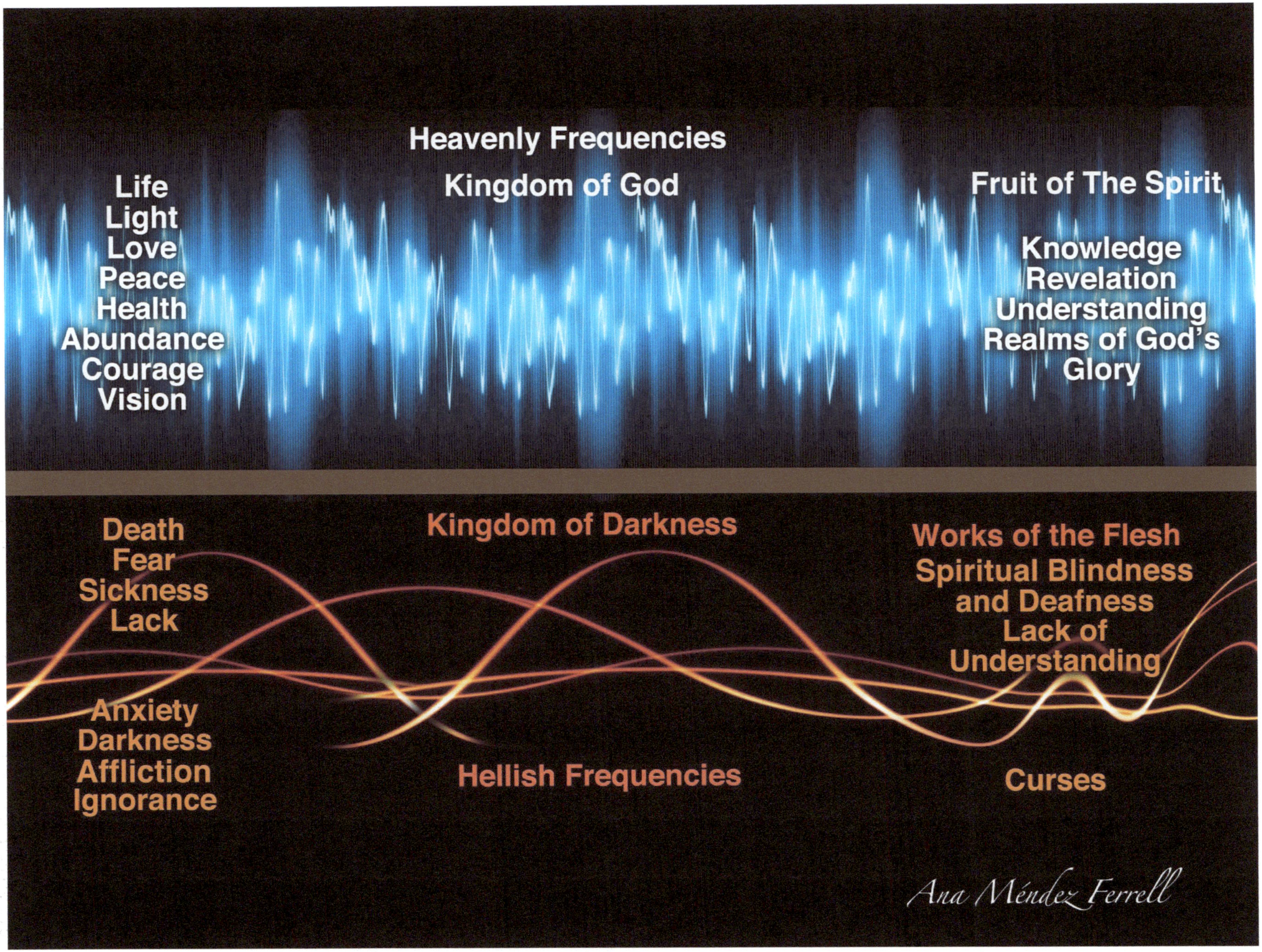

Heavenly Frequencies of the Kingdom of God

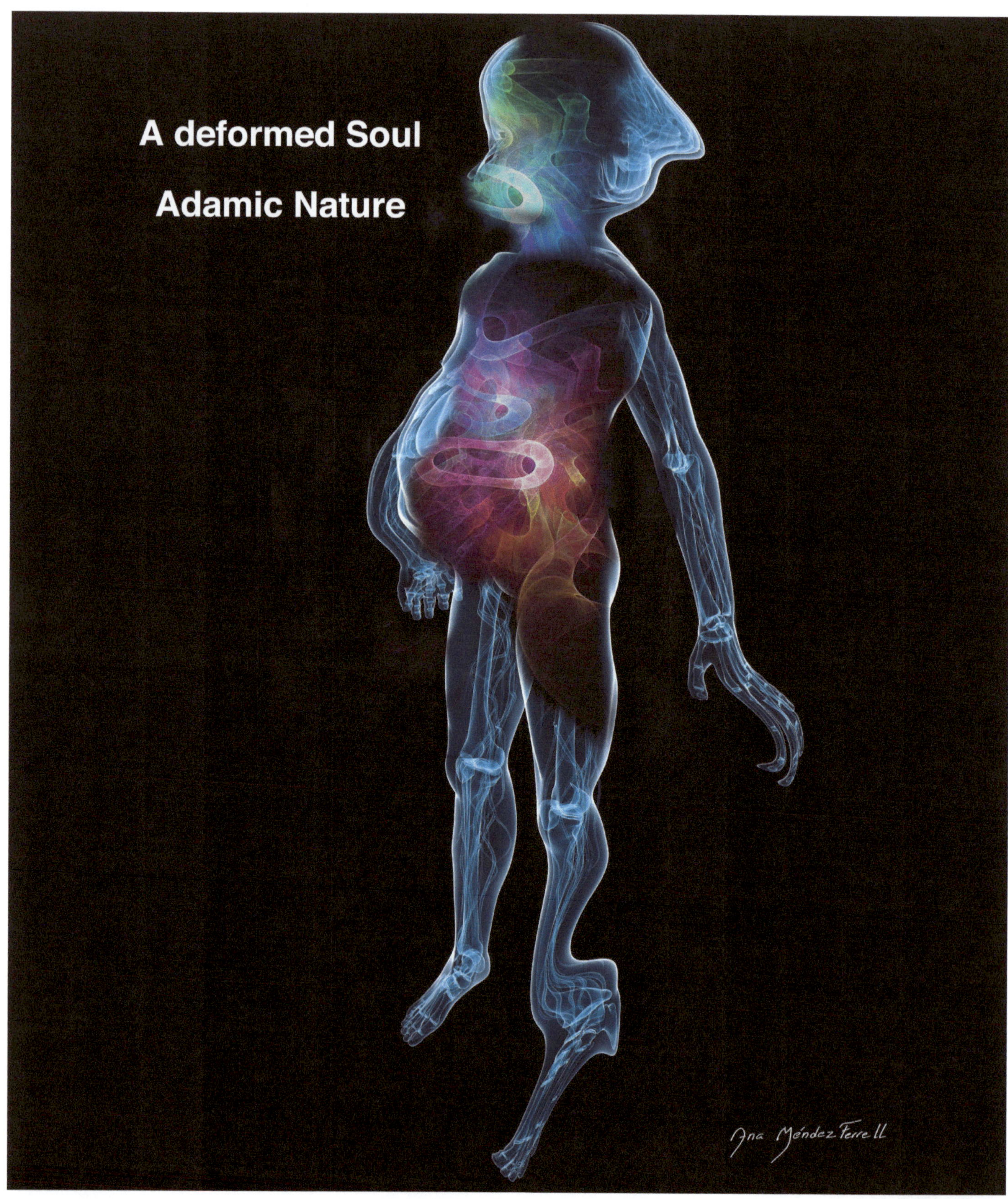

Deformed Soul Adamic Nature

MAIN NERVOUS PLEXUSES OF THE BODY

CARDIAC PLEXUS
CELIAC PLEXUS
SUPERIOR MESENTERIC PLEXUS
RENAL PLEXUS
ABDOMINAL AORTA
SMALL INTESTINE
AORTIC PLEXUS
AORTIC AND HYPOGASTRIC PLEXUSES
INFERIOR MESENTERIC PLEXUS
UPPER SACRAL GANGLION
VESICAL PLEXUS
RECTUM HYPOGASTRIC PLEXUS
SPERMATIC PLEXUS
Ana Méndez Ferrell

The Plexuses

Instruments of Oppression

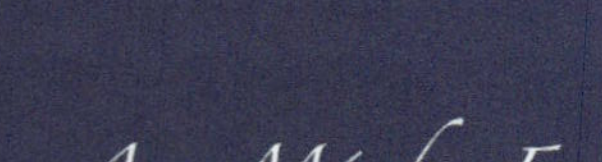

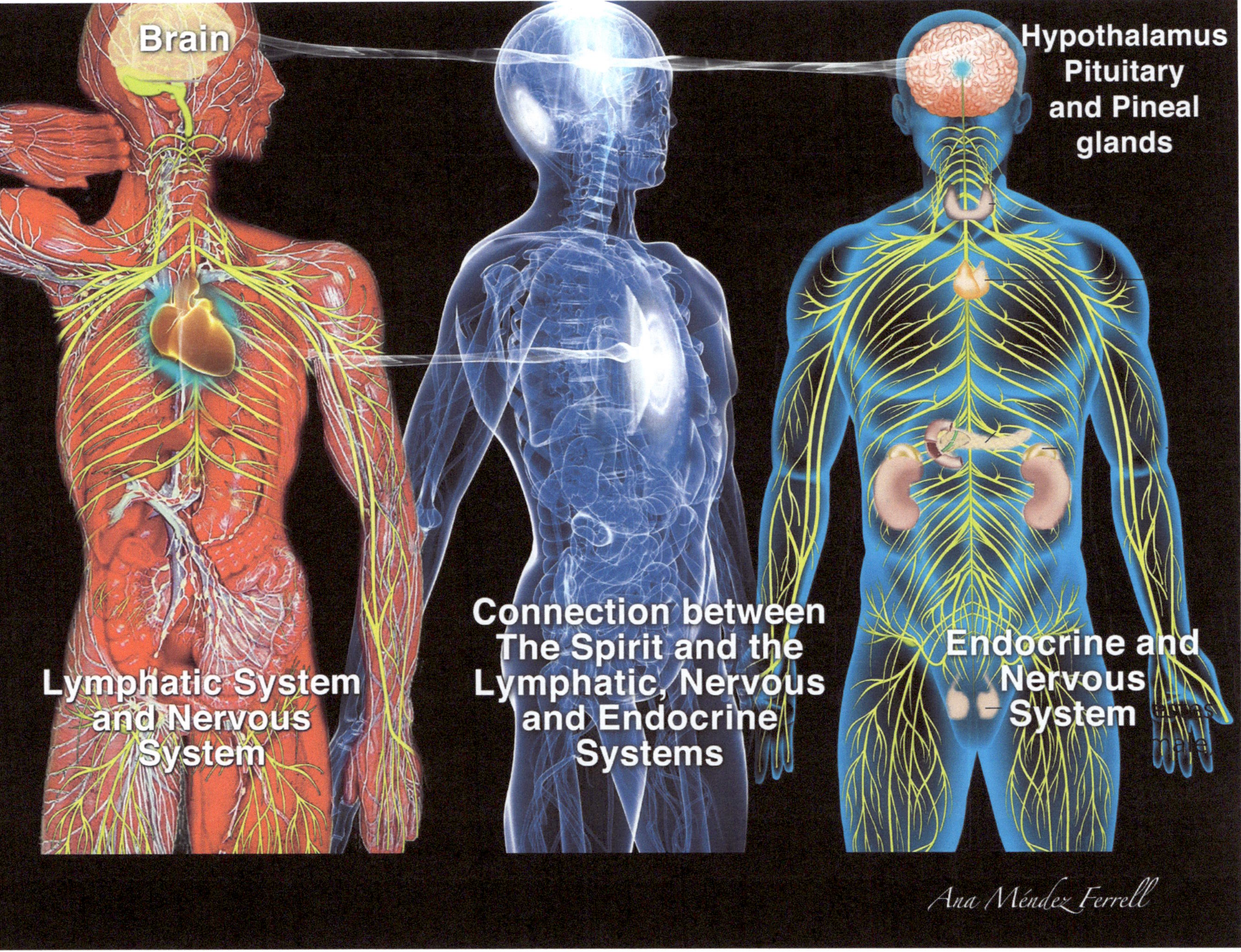

Connection Between the Spirit and Internal Systems

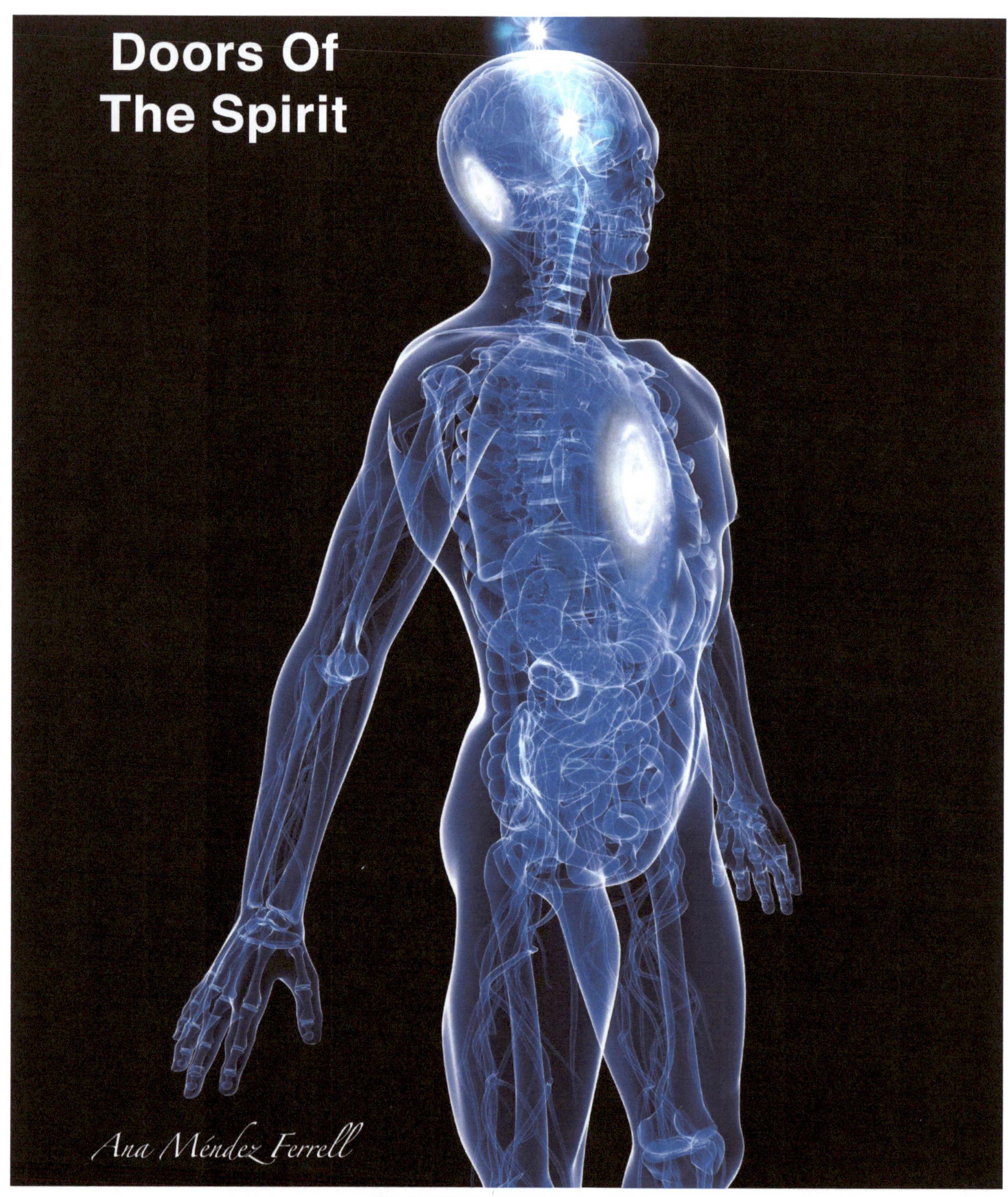
Doors Of
The Spirit
Ana Méndez Ferrell

www.ingramcontent.com/pod-product-compliance
Lightning Source LLC
LaVergne TN
LVHW070207110826
845147LV00002B/526